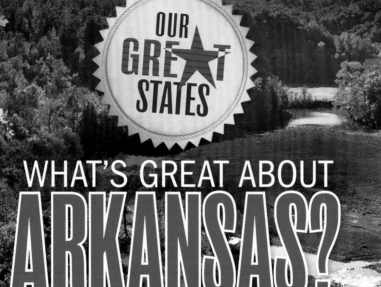

OUR
GRE★T
STATES

WHAT'S GREAT ABOUT
ARKANSAS?

✳ Darice Bailer

⌐ LERNER PUBLICATIONS COMPANY ✳ MINNEAPOLIS

CONTENTS

Content Consultant: Charles F. Robinson, Professor of History, University of Kansas

Lerner Publications Company
A division of Lerner Publishing Group, Inc.
241 First Avenue North
Minneapolis, MN 55401 USA

For reading levels and more information, look up this title at www.lernerbooks.com.

Main body text set in ITC Franklin Gothic Std Book Condensed 12/15.
Typeface provided by Adobe Systems.

Library of Congress Cataloging-in-Publication Data

Bailer, Darice.
    What's great about Arkansas? / by Darice Bailer.
        pages cm. — (Our great states)
    Includes index.
    ISBN 978-1-4677-3345-8 (lib. bdg. : alk. paper)
    ISBN 978-1-4677-4705-9 (eBook)
    1. Arkansas—Juvenile literature.
2. Arkansas—Guidebooks—Juvenile literature. I. Title. II. Title: What is great about Arkansas?
    F411.3.B295 2015
    976.7—dc23   2013050246

Manufactured in the United States of America
1 - PC - 7/15/14

ARKANSAS Welcomes You!

Arkansas is a place like no other! Imagine digging for diamonds and getting to keep your findings. Or watching cowboys ride bucking bulls at a rodeo. Maybe you are floating down the first US nationally protected river. You will find all of this and more in Arkansas. More than half of Arkansas is covered by forest. Lace up your shoes and run through the wooded trails. Or speed through the trees on a zip line. Find an underground cave to explore. Maybe saber-toothed tigers once lived there. Read on to discover ten cool places for you to visit and enjoy. Welcome to Arkansas, the Natural State!

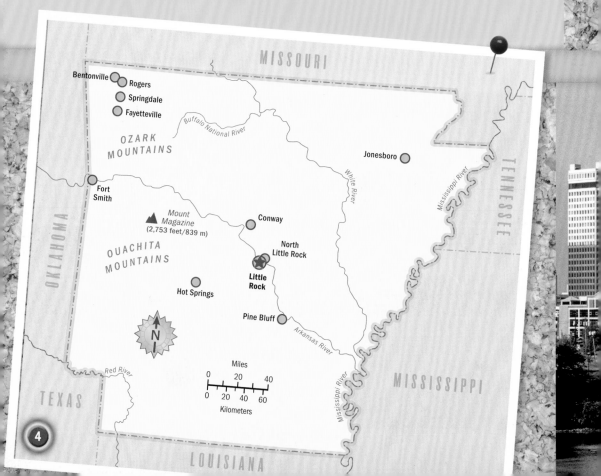

Explore Arkansas's forests
and all the places in between!
Just turn the page to
find out about
the NATURAL STATE. >

HOT SPRINGS

> You will want to stop in Hot Springs during your visit to Arkansas. Visit Hot Springs National Park and step back in time. Beginning in the early 1830s, people visited Hot Springs to take baths. Here, hot water bubbles up from deep inside the earth to form natural springs. The town used to bring the hot water into bathhouses. Many people visited for health reasons. The bathhouses were like spas.

Hot Springs is the oldest US national park. Walk down Bathhouse Row to visit eight old bathhouses. Take a tour and watch videos about historic Hot Springs. You can even enjoy a relaxing bath!

Ever ride a duck? You can in Hot Springs! A duck is a nickname for a bus that travels on land and on water. The National Park Duck Tour drives you down the streets of Hot Springs. Then it slips into Lake Hamilton.

Don't forget to visit the National Park Aquarium. You can see more than three hundred animals. Be on the lookout for a brown tortoise named Slow Poke. He enjoys following kids around the aquarium!

You will see historic equipment on your tour of the bathhouses.

QUAPAW BATHS

Natural hot springs have made the town of Hot Springs a popular tourist spot.

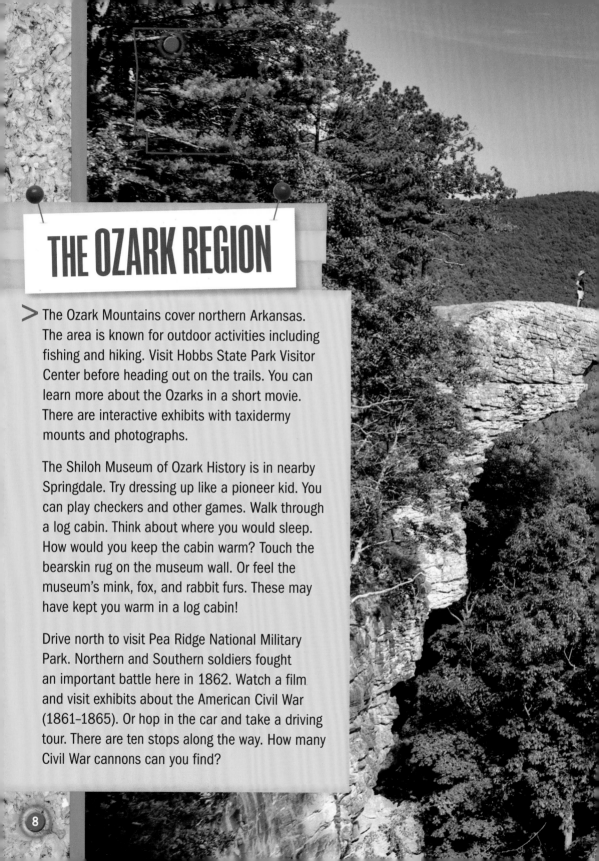

THE OZARK REGION

> The Ozark Mountains cover northern Arkansas. The area is known for outdoor activities including fishing and hiking. Visit Hobbs State Park Visitor Center before heading out on the trails. You can learn more about the Ozarks in a short movie. There are interactive exhibits with taxidermy mounts and photographs.

The Shiloh Museum of Ozark History is in nearby Springdale. Try dressing up like a pioneer kid. You can play checkers and other games. Walk through a log cabin. Think about where you would sleep. How would you keep the cabin warm? Touch the bearskin rug on the museum wall. Or feel the museum's mink, fox, and rabbit furs. These may have kept you warm in a log cabin!

Drive north to visit Pea Ridge National Military Park. Northern and Southern soldiers fought an important battle here in 1862. Watch a film and visit exhibits about the American Civil War (1861–1865). Or hop in the car and take a driving tour. There are ten stops along the way. How many Civil War cannons can you find?

AMERICAN CIVIL WAR

The American Civil War was fought between the Northern states and the Southern states. The North was called the Union. The South was called the Confederacy. Arkansas joined the Confederacy. The Union wanted to end slavery in the United States. Some battles happened in Arkansas.

Pea Ridge National Military Park has many exhibits and battle artifacts to see.

RODEO OF THE OZARKS

> Have you ever seen a cowboy ride a bucking bronco? Or seen someone rope a calf? Put your cowboy boots on and head to Rodeo of the Ozarks. It is held each July in Springdale. It is one of the largest outdoor rodeos in the world.

Watch marching bands, clowns, and horses in the parades. At night, make sure to watch the Mutton Bustin' competition. Mutton is sheep meat. You will see young cowboys and cowgirls riding sheep. They try to hold on as long as they can.

The rodeo even has a Goat Dressing Team Competition for kids. They try to put a pair of boxer shorts on a goat. The fastest team wins a prize!

Don't miss the professional bull riding. It is one of the most exciting events of the evening. The gate opens, and a bull bursts out. It may sound easy to stay on a bull for eight seconds, but think again! Watch the cowboys try to stay on the longest.

Cowboys get a bull ready for riding at a rodeo.

FARM CRED
MIDSOUTH

and Real Estate L
2-2817 Jonesboro, A

11

OZARK FOLK CENTER STATE PARK

> Be sure to stop at the Ozark Folk Center State Park. This park shares what it was like to be a pioneer living in the Ozarks. Watch different pioneer crafts being made. You can see dolls made from cornhusks. Or watch pottery being shaped on a wheel. Visit the town blacksmith. You can watch him shape iron into horseshoes. If you get hungry, stop at the Country Kitchen. Ready to help with the chores? Head over to the Folk Kids Mountain Garden. See if you can push the plow through the dirt!

The park also shows how pioneers had fun. Try walking around on an old pair of wooden stilts. Have a contest to see who can stand up longer! Go for a ride on an old merry-go-round. A mule pulls it!

End your day at the park's Loco Ropes Treetop Adventure Park. Try more than thirty challenges, including the Flying Pig ZipLine. It is a 300-foot (91-meter) ride through the forest.

See a woman making soap (*above*) or visit the wood-carver (*left*) and see him create wooden figurines.

BLANCHARD SPRINGS
CAVERNS

> Explore life belowground at the Blanchard Springs Caverns. You will see rocks dripping from the ceiling. These are called stalactites. You will also see stalagmites. These rocks grow from the ground. The cave's rock formations were carved millions of years ago! Run your fingers over the cool limestone. See if you can spot a salamander or a cricket crawling around. Maybe you will see saber-toothed tiger bones!

You can take different tours at Blanchard Springs Caverns. The US Forest Service guides will lead you on your tours. You will need to fit through some tight spots in the water-carved passages. The guides share stories about cave explorers. Early explorers dangled from ropes on homemade harnesses. Outlaws hid in these caves. The guides will tell ghost tales too. If one tour is not enough, join another tour!

Some group tours take visitors through narrow spaces in the caverns.

FORT SMITH

> In 1817, the US Army built Fort Smith on the Arkansas-Oklahoma border. It was built to keep peace between American Indian peoples. Fort Smith is now a national park.

Parts of the original Fort Smith are still standing. Start your day in the Visitors Center. It is the old courthouse, jail, and barracks. Learn about outlaws in the 1800s. You can also watch videos on military history. Other exhibits focus on the Trail of Tears. American Indians were forced to move west. Their path became known as the Trail of Tears. The US government made them move.

Keep following the path to the Trail of Tears Overlook. Fort Smith was the end of the trail for some routes. You can walk on the same path American Indians took.

After visiting the national park, stop in the town of Fort Smith. Buy a trolley ticket at the Fort Smith Trolley Museum. Ride the old trolley through town. Make a stop at the Fort Smith Museum of History. Order an ice-cream sundae at the old-fashioned soda fountain inside.

You can visit Fort Smith National Cemetery and pay your respects to fallen soldiers.

TRAIL OF TEARS

The Indian Removal Act of 1830 forced thousands of American Indians to move west of Arkansas. They did not want to leave their ancestral homes. Their route west became known as the Trail of Tears. It was a hard journey. Many American Indians suffered and died.

CRATER OF DIAMONDS
STATE PARK

> If you are looking to dig for gems, stop at Crater of Diamonds State Park in Murfreesboro. It is the only diamond site in the world open to the public. The biggest diamond found in the United States was found at the park. The 40.23-carat diamond was found in 1924.

About two diamonds are found each day. Maybe you will get lucky and find one! You could dig up a white, yellow, or brown stone. You can also find agate and amethyst stones.

Be ready to get muddy. You can bring your own bucket and shovel to the park. If you find any diamonds or stones, you get to keep them! The park staff will help identify a stone if you find one. You can spend all day searching the 37.5-acre (15-hectare) field.

You may be lucky enough to find a diamond when you're digging!

DIAMOND MINES OF ARKANSAS

SUPPLEMENT OF THE NASHVILLE NEWS
NASHVILLE, ARK

THE DISCOVERY OF DIAMONDS

People have been traveling to Arkansas to mine for diamonds since the early 1900s.

LITTLE ROCK

> Stop in Little Rock if you are looking for big-city fun. Little Rock is on the Arkansas River. It is Arkansas's capital. Catch the River Rail Streetcar to ride through town. Take the streetcar to the Museum of Discovery. Climb the lighthouse. Make sure to check out the theater too.

Stop and visit the Hillary Rodham Clinton Children's Library. You can cook healthful food from the garden. Take a walk and learn names of plants and trees. Check out the library's theater. Help design a set or costumes. Or maybe you would like to help write a play or act. Drop by to help out, or sign up for a program.

After the library, walk or bike the Big Dam Bridge. It is seven stories high! The bridge will take you to North Little Rock. Stop at the Arkansas Sports Hall of Fame. This museum is for Arkansas sports. Look for pictures of Jerry Jones. He owns the Dallas Cowboys football team and grew up in North Little Rock. Pretend you are a sportscaster and record your own show!

THE LITTLE ROCK NINE

Until 1957, most Arkansas public schools were segregated. That meant African American students went to school separated from white students. In 1957, Little Rock Central High School had its first African American students. There were nine new students. They were nicknamed the Little Rock Nine. They were a big part of history. See their statues at the Arkansas State Capitol.

Hillary Rodham Clinton reads a story at the children's library and learning center named after her.

THE WILLIAM J. CLINTON LIBRARY & MUSEUM

> Former president William (Bill) Clinton grew up in Arkansas. The former governor of Arkansas became the forty-second president of the United States. You can visit his presidential library in Little Rock.

The US Secret Service protected the president and drove him around. One of the limousines they used is on the first floor of the museum.

The museum has a replica of the White House's Oval Office. You can sit in the president's old chair. Pretend you are president of the United States. Make sure to get your picture taken!

Pick up an Arkansas Passport at the museum store. Have it stamped before you leave. Take it with you to the Clinton Birthplace Museum in Hope. Bring it to Hot Springs where Clinton grew up. And take it to the Clinton House Museum in Fayetteville. This was Bill Clinton and Hillary Rodham Clinton's first home. They were also married here. Take a tour of their home. Fayetteville is also the home of the University of Arkansas. The Clintons both taught here at one time.

Peek inside one of Bill Clinton's presidential limousines while touring the museum.

MAYA ANGELOU

President Clinton asked Arkansas poet Maya Angelou to write a poem for him. She read it at his first inauguration in 1993. Angelou grew up in a little Arkansas town called Stamps. Angelou is one of the most famous American poets. She also writes books. In 1995, she set a record for a two-year run on *the New York Times*' paperback nonfiction best-seller list.

THE BUFFALO
NATIONAL RIVER

> The Buffalo National River is a treasure. It flows freely from beginning to end. This means there are no dams. River dams stop the water flow. There are few rivers in the world that have no dams. President Richard Nixon made this waterway a national river in 1972. It was the first national river in the country.

Start at the Tyler Bend Visitor Center in Saint Joe. Paddle along in a kayak or a canoe to see the trees and bluffs. Look out for elk. Approximately 450 elk live along the river. Did you know elk disappeared from Arkansas for nearly one hundred years? The Ponca Elk Education Center will tell you why this animal disappeared.

Hunt for crayfish under rocks. See who can skip a pebble the farthest. Spread a blanket and enjoy a picnic. Join a park ranger for a tour. The ranger can show you what animals live near the river. Hike the trails with or without a ranger. Go horseback riding on Old River Trail. Tired? Camp out at one of many campgrounds. Count the stars and the croaking frogs as you fall asleep.

YOUR TOP TEN!

You have read about ten awesome things to do and see in Arkansas. What would your top ten list include? What would you like to see and do if you visited the Natural State? What attraction has you most excited? These are all things to think about as you write your own top ten. Write down your top ten list on a separate sheet of paper. Turn your list into a book. Illustrate it with drawings or pictures from magazines or the Internet.

It is common to see elk along the banks of the Buffalo River.

⭐ Capital city

◯ City

◯ Point of interest

▲ Highest elevation

—·— State border

ARKANSAS

Visit www.lerneresource.com to learn
more about the state flag of Arkansas.

ARKANSAS BY MAP

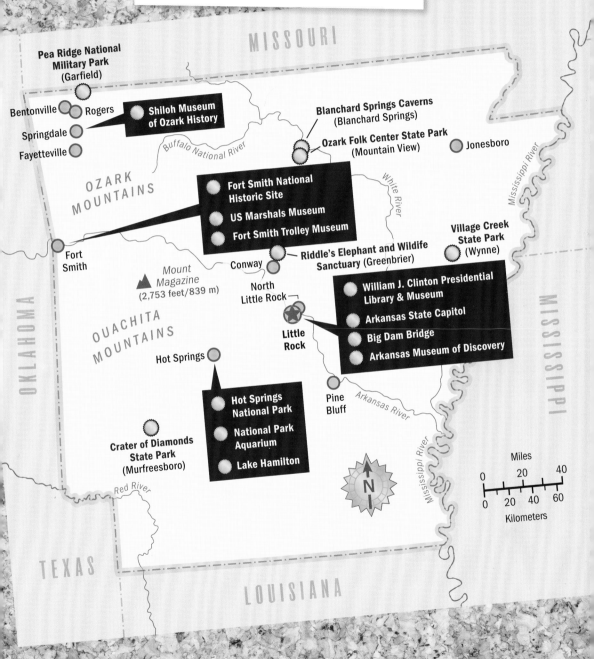

MISSOURI

Pea Ridge National
Military Park
(Garfield)

Bentonville

Rogers

Springdale

Fayetteville

Shiloh Museum
of Ozark History

Buffalo National River

Blanchard Springs Caverns
(Blanchard Springs)

Ozark Folk Center State Park
(Mountain View)

Jonesboro

White River

Mississippi River

OZARK
MOUNTAINS

Fort Smith National
Historic Site

US Marshals Museum

Fort Smith Trolley Museum

Fort
Smith

Conway

Riddle's Elephant and Wildlife
Sanctuary (Greenbrier)

Village Creek
State Park
(Wynne)

Mount
Magazine
(2,753 feet/839 m)

North
Little Rock

OUACHITA
MOUNTAINS

OKLAHOMA

Little
Rock

William J. Clinton Presidential
Library & Museum

Arkansas State Capitol

Big Dam Bridge

Arkansas Museum of Discovery

MISSISSIPPI

Hot Springs

Pine
Bluff

Arkansas River

Crater of Diamonds
State Park
(Murfreesboro)

Hot Springs
National Park

National Park
Aquarium

Lake Hamilton

Red River

Mississippi River

N

Miles
0   20   40

0   20   40   60
Kilometers

TEXAS

LOUISIANA

ARKANSAS FACTS

NICKNAME: The Natural State

SONGS: "Arkansas (You Run Deep in Me)" by Wayland Holyfield

MOTTO: *Regnat Populus* or "The people rule"

> **FLOWER:** apple blossom

TREE: loblolly pine

BIRD: mockingbird

ANIMAL: white-tailed deer

> **FOOD:** rice

DATE AND RANK OF STATEHOOD: June 15, 1836; the 25th state

> **CAPITAL:** Little Rock

AREA: 53,180 square miles (137,736 sq. km)

AVERAGE JANUARY TEMPERATURE: 41°F (5°C)

AVERAGE JULY TEMPERATURE: 83°F (28°C)

POPULATION AND RANK: 2,949,131; 32nd

MAJOR CITIES AND POPULATIONS: Little Rock (193,524), Fort Smith (86,209), Fayetteville (73,580), Springdale (69,797), Jonesboro (67,263)

NUMBER OF US CONGRESS MEMBERS: 4 representatives, 2 senators

NUMBER OF ELECTORAL VOTES: 6

NATURAL RESOURCES: petroleum, natural gas, coal, silica stone, diamonds, quartz crystal

> **AGRICULTURAL PRODUCTS:** rice, poultry, grain, soybeans, cotton, corn, tomatoes

MANUFACTURED GOODS: paper products, chemicals, electric motors, appliances, plastic and rubber products, wood

GLOSSARY

ancestral: from someone's ancestors (people in the family who lived a long time ago)

crayfish: a small animal that lives in fresh water and is related to the lobster

dam: a barrier preventing the flow of water

inauguration: a ceremony introducing a person into office

interactive: involving the actions of a user

limestone: a rock formed from animal remains such as shells or coral

limousine: a large car often driven by a chauffeur

pioneer: one of the first to settle in an area

replica: a copy exact in all its details

rodeo: a contest of cowboy skills

spa: a place where people go to improve their health and appearance through exercising and relaxing

stilt: a pole with a strap for the foot used so a person can walk high above the ground

taxidermy: the skill of preparing, stuffing, and mounting skins of animals

LERNER

SOURCE™

Expand learning beyond the printed book. Download free, complementary educational resources for this book from our website, www.lernerresource.com.

FURTHER INFORMATION

Activities in Little Rock
http://www.savvykidsofarkansas.com
What can a kid do in Little Rock? Start with breakfast with the animals at the Little Rock Zoo or the new robots exhibit at Little Rock's Museum of Discovery! Savvy Kids points out the fun.

Arkansas for Kids
http://www.arkansas.com/kids
Find cool facts, word searches, online puzzles, and games! You can also discover a fun place to go, or you can read about a famous Arkansan.

The Encyclopedia of Arkansas
http://www.encyclopediaofarkansas.net
The Encyclopedia of Arkansas History & Culture has all the information you need to write a report about Arkansas. Find out more about Arkansas's geography, American Indians, European explorers, and more.

McPherson, Stephanie Sammartino. *Bill Clinton*. Minneapolis: Lerner Publications, 2008. Read about Bill Clinton's early childhood in Arkansas and how he grew up to become the fortieth and forty-second governor of Arkansas and the forty-second president of the United States.

Prentzas, G.S. *Arkansas*. New York: Children's Press, 2014. This book includes everything you want to know about Arkansas, from its early explorers to the famous people who call this state home. In addition to chapters on history and government, there is a travel guide to point out the parks, the museums, and the festivals you will want to see.

Shoulders, Michael. *N Is for Natural State: An Arkansas Alphabet*. Ann Arbor, MI: Sleeping Bear Press, 2003. This selection covers Arkansas from *A* to *Z*! Begin your journey with *A*, and discover how American Indians helped give Arkansas its name.

INDEX

PHOTO ACKNOWLEDGMENTS

The images in this book are used with the permission of: © Brandon Alms/Shutterstock Images, p. 1; © Spirit of America/Shutterstock Images, pp. 4–5, 22–23, 22; © Laura Westlund/Independent Picture Service, p. 4, 27; © Warren Price Photography/iStockphoto, p. 5; © Lori Martin/Shutterstock Images, pp. 6–7; © Zack Frank/Shutterstock Images, p. 7 (top); © rarena/Shutterstock Images, p. 7 (bottom); © ABDESIGN/iStockphoto, pp. 8–9; © Ric Ergenbright/Corbis, p. 9 (top); Library of Congress, pp. 9 (bottom) (LC-USZC4-1330), 20 (LC-DIG-highsm-12881); © The Jonesboro Sun/Krystin McClellan/AP Images, pp. 10–11; © PicWorks/iStockphoto, p. 10; © William A. Bake/Corbis, pp. 12–13; © Bob Krist/Corbis, p. 13 (left); © Buddy Mays/Corbis, p. 13 (right); © iStockphoto/Thinkstock, pp. 14–15, 16–17; © Mike Wintroath/AP Images, p. 14; © SuperStock/Glow Images, p. 17 (top); National Park Service, p. 17 (bottom); © Jessica Rinaldi/Reuters/Corbis, pp. 18–19; © Arkansas State Parks/AP Images, p. 19 (top); American Museum of Natural History, p. 19 (bottom); © dlewis33/iStockphoto, pp. 20–21, 24–25; © Danny Johnston/AP Images, p. 21; © NPR/White House, p. 23; © jcrader/iStockphoto, p. 25; © nicoolay/iStockphoto, p. 26; © boboling/iStockphoto, p. 29 (top); © joel-t/iStockphoto, p. 29 (middle top); © Davel5957/iStockphoto, p. 29 (middle bottom); © pkripper503/iStockphoto, p. 29 (bottom).

Front cover: Front Cover: Cover: © Panoramic Images/Getty Images, (cave); © iStockphoto.com/Davel5957, (skyline); © iStockphoto.com/Steve Byland, (razorback); © Laura Westlund/Independent Picture Service (map); © iStockphoto.com/fpm (seal); © iStockphoto.com/vicm (pushpins); © iStockphoto.com/benz190 (corkboard).